IMPROVING MARKING AND REPORTING IN CLASSROOM INSTRUCTION

A Title in the CURRENT TOPICS
IN CLASSROOM INSTRUCTION Series

Norman E. Gronlund

Professor of Educational Psychology
University of Illinois

Macmillan Publishing Co., Inc.
New York
Collier Macmillan Publishers,
London

To Jim and Edna

Macmillan Publishing Co., Inc.
866 Third Avenue, New York, New York 10022

Collier-Macmillan Canada, Ltd.

Library of Congress Cataloging in Publication Data
Gronlund, Norman Edward, (date)
  Improving marking and reporting in classroom instruction.

  (Current topics in classroom instruction series)
  Includes bibliographical references.
  1. Grading and marking (Students) I. Title.
LB3051.G735   371.2'72   74-1082
ISBN 0-02-348140-4

Printing: 1 2 3 4 5 6 7 8   Year: 4 5 6 7 8 9 0

Preface

The improvement of marking and reporting practices is always of current interest to educators. It has been a persistent topic of discussion in the professional literature for more than fifty years and is a problem of perennial interest to parents, students, teachers, and other school personnel. Many suggestions for improvement in marking and reporting have been offered, but changes in marking practices have been gradual and relatively minor. The problems of marking and reporting remain unresolved for many reasons. Two of the more important reasons are: (1) the focus typically has been on how to develop a *single* marking system (e.g., A, B, C, D, F grades) that will serve the diverse needs of students, parents, teachers, counselors, and school administrators, and (2) efforts to improve marking and reporting typically have been directed toward the manipulation of the symbols used (e.g., substituting S, U for A, B, C, D, F) rather than toward the basic issues involved.

A marking and reporting system is simply a means of communicating student learning progress to others. It is an integral part of the teaching-learning process, however, and cannot, therefore, be separated from the other functions of the instructional program. Effective reporting depends on effective evaluation, and effective evaluation depends on a clear conception of the intended learning outcomes. Thus, although our focus in this book is on how to improve marking and reporting practices, we are assuming that the school program is based on clearly defined objectives and sound testing and evaluation procedures. Unless this is the case, no marking and reporting system can be expected to effectively serve its intended functions.

This book is intended as a practical guide for the preservice and in-service education of teachers. The first chapter describes current practices in marking and reporting student progress. This is followed by guidelines for improving marking and reporting systems (Chapter 2), methods of assigning norm-referenced letter grades (Chapter 3), the use of criterion-referenced marking and reporting practices (Chapter 4), and procedures for effective parent-teacher conferences (Chapter 5). The appendix includes a check list for evaluating a marking and reporting system, a sample parent-teacher conference guide, and a list of references.

Special appreciation is expressed to publishers and schools for permitting the use of their illustrative materials. The efficient typing services of Marian Brinkerhoff are also gratefully acknowledged.

N. E. G.

Contents

Chapter

1   Current Practices in Marking and Reporting   1

Current Marking and Reporting Practices   2
Report Cards in Current Use   3
Advantages and Limitations of Current Practices   5
Current Trends in Marking and Reporting   7

2   Guidelines for Improving Marking and Reporting   9

Functions of Marking and Reporting Systems   10
Factors to Be Included in School Marks and
    Reports   13
Frames of Reference for Judging Student
    Performance   14
Types of Report Forms   16
Guidelines for Improving Marking and Reporting   19

3   Assigning Norm-Referenced Letter Grades   21

Letter Grades as Valid Indicators of Achievement   22
Combining Data in Assigning Grades   23
Determining the Distribution of Grades   25
Supplementing Norm-Referenced Letter Grades   27

4   Criterion-Referenced Marking and Reporting   29

Conventional Grading with Absolute Standards   31
Criterion-Referenced Reporting and Mastery
    Learning   32
Criterion-Referenced Reporting and Individualized
    Instruction   35

5   Parent-Teacher Conferences   38
            Preparing for the Conference   39
            Conducting the Conference   40
            Some Important Conference "Don'ts"   43
            Reporting Standardized Test Results to Parents   44

Appendix A.   Check List for Evaluating a Marking and Reporting
                 System   49

Appendix B.   Sample Parent-Teacher Conference Guide   51

Appendix C.   References   56

Index   58

List of Figures

1.   Comprehensive Elementary School Report Form   17

2.   High School Report Form Illustrating a Multiple-Marking
        System   18

3.   Normal Curve with a Typical Distribution of Grades   26

4.   Report Form Used with a Mastery Learning Approach   34

5.   Goal Card for Reporting Individual Progress   36

6.   Percentage of Students at Each Stanine Level   46

Chapter 1
Current Practices in Marking and Reporting

Most classroom teachers would rank the problem of marking and reporting student learning progress near the top of any list of issues of major concern to them. They view the assigning of marks, or the preparation of progress reports, as one of the most frustrating aspects of teaching. Many teachers have been heard to say, "I enjoy teaching but I dread reporting time."

Much of the frustration connected with marking and reporting results from the fact that the process involves so many subjective judgments and there are so few specific guidelines to aid teachers in making the judgments. For example, the types of issues that must be considered in assigning single letter grades (e.g., A, B, C, D, F) as indicators of student learning would include such considerations as the following:

1. Should the grade represent student achievement only or should it also include the student's effort and work habits?
2. What types of student achievement (e.g., test scores, written work, performance skills, etc.) should be included in the grade?
3. How should the various elements of achievement and development be weighted?
4. Should the grade represent relative achievement or some absolute level of performance?
5. What distribution of grades (i.e., A, B, C, D, F) should be used and how should this distribution be determined?

Although some schools have policies that serve as guidelines for some of these issues, the burden of judgment usually rests on the teacher. It is he who must, in the final analysis, make the decisions and combine the diverse elements of student performance into a single letter grade.

As we shall see shortly, some schools have moved from the single letter grade to other methods of marking and reporting. This however, has not relieved the teacher of the burden of making judgments. It simply has changed the types of judgments that the teacher must make. All marking and reporting systems are based on teachers' judgments of student performance. There is no way to avoid these judgments. All we can reasonably expect to do is to provide guidelines that will make the task less frustrating and burdensome to the teacher and make the reports more valid and useful to students, parents, and school personnel. We propose to do this (1) by describing methods for improving the marking and reporting system, and (2) by providing suggestions for the more effective use of present marking and reporting practices. But first let us take a look at the practices that are currently being used in the schools.

Current Marking and Reporting Practices

Reports of student learning progress typically take one of the following forms:

> Traditional Report Cards (e.g., A, B, C, D, F)
> Letters or written reports
> Parent-teacher conferences

On report cards, some schools use numbers (e.g., 1, 2, 3, 4, 5) in place of letter grades and other schools use fewer letters than the traditional five (e.g., O = outstanding, S = satisfactory, and N = needs improvement). Still other schools confine the marking to a simple pass-fail or satisfactory-unsatisfactory scale. Despite these variations, the use of traditional letter grades (A, B, C, D, F) is still the most common method of marking, and report cards using these letters constitute the most widely used method of reporting student progress.

Several years ago the Research Division of the National Education Association made a nationwide sample survey of the marking and reporting practices used by public-school teachers (NEA, 1970). Their findings, shown in Table I, indicate the prominent place that letter grades hold in reporting student progress. Letter grades are still used in the majority of schools, at both the elementary and secondary levels, despite the fact that they have been under almost constant criticism for the past fifty years. The continued use of letter grades would seem to suggest that they are serving some useful purpose (e.g., administrative functions) or that they are so deeply embedded in our total institutional culture (Thorndike, 1969) that their modification or replacement is strongly resisted. In either case, our best approach would seem to be the improvement of the letter grade system and the *supplementing* of letter grades with more detailed and meaningful reports of student learning.

The fact that the percentages in Table I total more than one hundred indicates that some teachers used more than one reporting method. This would seem to be a desirable practice. A single reporting method can hardly be expected to serve the diverse needs of students, parents, teachers, counselors,

Table I.   Percentage of Teachers Using Each Method in
Reporting Student Progress to Parents*

Method of Reporting	Elementary Teachers	Secondary Teachers
Letter grades (e.g., A, B, C, D, F)	72%	83%**
Parent-teacher conferences	60	20
Written descriptions of performance	24	10
Number grades (e.g, 1, 2, 3, 4, 5)	10	9
Percentage grades	2	10
Pass-fail reports	8	3

*Adapted from nationwide sample survey of public school teachers (NEA Research Division, 1970).

**Percentages were rounded to nearest whole per cent.

and school administrators. Our attempts to make one type of progress report serve the needs of all interested users probably underlies much of the criticism leveled at any one particular method.

As would be expected, a larger percentage of elementary than of secondary teachers report using conferences with parents and written descriptions of student performance. The smaller number of students that teachers have to report on makes these reporting methods more feasible at the elementary level. Closer contacts with parents and more detailed reports on the learning and development of children are also probably more necessary during the earlier stages of schooling. Parent-teacher conferences, for example, make it possible for the teacher to share information with parents and to secure their cooperation in fostering the total development of children during these formative years.

Report Cards in Current Use

As previously noted, the report card is still the primary method of reporting student progress. The typical report card includes a place to mark achievement in each subject (e.g., A, B, C, D, F) and a place to check a series of work habits and other personal and social characteristics. Some report cards include a check list of objectives for each subject instead of the single letter grade. The following statements for elementary school mathematics illustrate this type of report.

MATHEMATICS

1. Knows basic number facts.
2. Understands mathematical concepts.
3. Uses fundamental processes with accuracy.
4. Reasons well in problem solving.

Student performance on each objective is typically indicated by checking whether the student's learning progress is satisfactory or improvement is needed.

Current practice in reporting achievement on elementary school report cards is shown in Table II. This table is based on a survey of 100 school districts in all fifty states, by Mousley (1972).

Table II. Percentage of 100 School Districts Using Each Method of
Reporting Achievement on Elementary-School Report Cards*

Method of Reporting	Grades 1–3	Grades 4–6
Letter grades (e.g., A, B, C, D, F)	62%	86%
Three letters (e.g., O, S, N)	14	4
Two letters (e.g., Pass-Fail)	10	4
Number grades (e.g., 1, 2, 3, 4, 5)	1	4
Check lists of objectives	13	2

*Adapted from Mousley (1972).

The results presented in Table II are consistent with the NEA study, presented earlier, in showing that the traditional letter grade (A, B, C, D, F) is the dominant method of reporting student progress. Although it is used less frequently in grades 1-3, it is still used by almost two thirds of the school districts at that level.

The use of two or three letters, in place of the traditional five letter system, has achieved some popularity in elementary schools. Their greater use in grades 1-3 is probably the result of attempts to de-emphasize competitive grading at the primary level.

Especially disappointing is the infrequent use of check lists of objectives for reporting achievement. More than twenty-five years ago, Wrinkle made an eloquent plea for reporting achievement in terms of behaviorally stated objectives. His book entitled *Improving Marking and Reporting Practices* (1947) was widely read and has been quoted in numerous educational measurement and educational methods textbooks over the years. Despite this widespread attention to the advantages of using check lists of objectives, relatively few schools have adopted the practice. The present resurgence of interest in stating instructional objectives in behavioral, or measurable, terms for instructional purposes (Gronlund, 1970), however, can be expected to create a new demand for incorporating them into the marking and reporting system. It would seem educationally unsound to use behaviorally stated objectives for instructional and evaluation purposes and not to use them in reports of student progress.

A survey of the marking practices of 3,800 secondary school teachers has shown that 96 per cent use either a five category system (e.g., A, B, C, D, F) or a percentage grade (Terwilliger, 1966). These findings are in harmony with the NEA survey presented in Table I and indicate that report cards at the secondary level are likely to show less variation than those at the elementary level. The demand for letter grades and the resulting grade point average, by college admissions officers, probably contributes to the greater uniformity of marking practices at the secondary level.

Advantages and Limitations of Current Practices

None of the marking and reporting practices in current use are completely satisfactory. That is one of the reasons that we have so many different marking and reporting systems. The following advantages and limitations are commonly cited for each of the methods.

TRADITIONAL LETTER GRADES (A, B, C, D, F)

Advantages
1. Easy to use and convenient in maintaining school records
2. Can be easily averaged for administrative uses.
3. Are *apparently* easy to interpret.
4. Provide fairly good predictions of future achievement;

Limitations
1. Meaning of a letter grade (e.g., B) varies from school to school and from teacher to teacher.
2. Letter grades typically reflect a conglomerate of achievement, effort, and personal behavior.
3. Letter grades provide a system of unfair competition among students.
4. Letter grades become ends in themselves, rather than serve as means to an end.
5. Letter grades produce harmful side effects (e.g., anxiety, cheating, poor self-concept).
6. Letter grades do *not* indicate a student's learning strengths and weaknesses.

PASS-FAIL SYSTEM

Advantages
1. Easy to use and record.
2. Removes the competitive pressures of letter grading.
3. Permits students to explore new subject areas without fear of low grades.

Limitations
1. Provides even less information about student learning than the traditional letter grades.
2. A two-category system is less reliable than a five-category system.

3. Study effort may be directed toward merely passing rather than obtaining a higher level of performance.
4. The value of grades for predicting future achievement (e.g., success in college) is lost.

CHECK LISTS OF OBJECTIVES

Advantages
1. Provides a detailed analysis of learning strengths and weaknesses.
2. Keeps students and parents aware of the instructional goals of the school.
3. Can be used to detect weaknesses in the instructional program (e.g., unattained objectives).

Limitations
1. More time consuming to prepare the reports.
2. Statements of objectives are not readily understood by parents with little education.
3. Reporting system must be changed when the basic set of instructional objectives is changed.

LETTERS TO PARENTS

Advantages
1. Provides for a highly individualized report of learning strengths and weaknesses.
2. Permits teachers to focus on those learning areas that are most essential to student progress at a particular time.
3. Permits teachers to describe the inter-relation of the student's development in different areas.

Limitations
1. Well-written letters are time consuming and difficult to write.
2. Written descriptions of student weaknesses are easily misinterpreted by parents.
3. Letters tend to deteriorate into generalized, stereotyped statements of little value.
4. Letters provide no systematic and cumulative record of student progress toward school goals.

PARENT-TEACHER CONFERENCE

Advantages
1. Flexible procedure that permits two-way communication.
2. More extensive reporting and interpretation of learning progress is possible.

3. Misunderstandings can be avoided, or overcome, through discussion.
4. Parent and teacher can develop a mutual understanding and a cooperative plan for improving the student's development.

Limitations
1. Extremely time consuming.
2. Requires special counseling skills that many teachers lack.
3. Many parents are unable, or unwilling, to come for conferences.
4. Inadequate student personnel records, or lack of access to them, limits the types of information teachers can share with parents.
5. Conferences are difficult to summarize for school records.

The advantages and limitations of the various methods of marking and reporting reflect the fact that each method serves some purposes well but serves other purposes not as well or poorly. For example, letter grades (A, B, C, D, F) provide a simplified system for keeping school records, pass-fail marking encourages the exploration of new areas of study, check lists of objectives provide a diagnostic report on students' learning strengths and weaknesses, and parent-teacher conferences encourage cooperation between home and school. Thus, rather than attempting to decide which marking and reporting method is best, we should concentrate on the development of a multiple marking and reporting system that utilizes the strengths of each particular method. This is the approach that is taken in the next chapter.

Current Trends in Marking and Reporting

A recent review of the research on marking and reporting by the National Education Association (NEA, 1970) has indicated that current practice is shifting toward:

1. The use of committees of students, parents, teachers, and other school personnel to improve marking and reporting practices.
2. The use of both report cards and parent-teacher conferences for reporting student progress (especially in elementary schools).
3. The use of report forms that are specifically adapted to particular grade levels.
4. The use of more detailed reports, such as behaviorally stated objectives for subject fields, social adjustment, personal development, and work habits.
5. The use of marking systems that compare a student's learning progress with his own potential (especially in elementary schools) as well as with the achievement of others.
6. The use of report cards that provide space for both teachers and parents comments.
7. The use of less frequent reporting (e.g., twice a year).

8. The use of student evaluation as an adjunct to teacher evaluation of learning progress.

In addition to these trends, that largely reflect the research of the 1960's and earlier, there has been a fairly recent trend in the use of the pass-fail option at the high school and college levels. With this system, students are typically permitted to take some courses under the pass-fail option to encourage them to explore new areas without fear of lowering their grade point average. The option of selecting a pass-fail grade is commonly restricted to elective courses and there is usually a limit on the number of courses that can be taken under pass-fail conditions.

Chapter 2
Guidelines for Improving Marking and Reporting

As noted in Chapter 1, current school practices in reporting student progress are diverse and varied. Although the majority of schools use traditional letter grades (A, B, C, D, F), other schools supplement or replace them with fewer letters (e.g., O, S, N or P, F), with number systems (e.g., 1, 2, 3, 4, 5), with check lists of objectives, with written descriptions, or with parent-teacher conferences. Some of this variation is probably due to the fact that no single reporting system can meet the varied needs of different localities and different grade levels. Some of it, however, is also due to the fact that many schools have not developed a definitive policy on the role of the marking and reporting system in the school program.

Without a clearly defined school policy, the improvement of the marking and reporting system often focuses on manipulation of the symbols used in marking. For example, five-letter grades are replaced by two-letter grades, letter grades are replaced by numbers, or pluses and minuses are added to the present letter grade system. No amount of shifting from one set of symbols to another, however, is going to basically improve the marking and reporting system. What is needed is a careful consideration of questions such as the following:

1. What functions are to be served by the marking and reporting system?
2. What aspects of student achievement and development should be included in school marks and reports?
3. What frame of reference (e.g., relative or absolute) should be used for judging student performance?
4. What type of marking and reporting form should be used?

Each of these issues is discussed in turn. This discussion is followed by a set of guidelines for developing and effective marking and reporting system.

Functions of Marking and Reporting Systems

Marking and reporting systems serve a number of functions in the school. These include (1) instructional functions, (2) information functions, (3) guidance functions, and (4) administrative functions.

Instructional Functions. The main goal of any instructional program is the improvement of student learning and development. The marking and reporting system can contribute to this effort if it is carefully developed and wisely used.

An effective reporting plan can provide systematic feedback to students concerning the extent to which the instructional objectives are being achieved. If the plan is sufficiently detailed, it can pinpoint the student's strengths and weaknesses in each area of study with implications for corrective action. Although students receive feedback from tests and other evaluations of their schoolwork during the teaching-learning process, the periodic report provides a more systematic and comprehensive summing up of learning progress. This is true, of course, only if the report includes more than a single letter grade for each subject.

The periodic report can also contribute to student motivation by providing the student with short-term goals. It is difficult for anyone to work for extended periods of time without some feedback concerning his progress. Whether or not the feedback is motivating depends to a large extent on the nature of the report and the attitude the teacher conveys to the students. If a single letter grade is used and teachers coerce students into working with the threat of a low mark, then the results are likely to be unsatisfactory. However, if a more elaborate report of learning strengths and weaknesses is used and the report is viewed as an opportunity to check on learning progress, quite different results are likely to ensue. When viewed in a positive light, marks indicating good progress toward course goals tend to reinforce learning and marks indicating inadequate progress can provide a stimulus to greater effort. Low marks are most likely to result in increased effort when they follow some positive evaluation of progress and when the report indicates the specific aspects of performance needing improvement.

In addition to having a direct influence on student learning and development, well-designed progress reports can contribute to the instructional program in other ways. They can be used by teachers, for example, in planning remedial work, in helping students select courses or other specific learning experiences, and in assisting students to develop realistic appraisals of their strengths and weaknesses. They can also contribute to an evaluation of the instructional program by identifying content or skill areas that are causing a majority of the students difficulty. This might suggest needed revision in particular instructional objectives, in the learning activities, or in both. Thus, carefully developed reports of student progress can contribute to the teaching-learning process in a number of important ways.

For instructional purposes, the most useful type of report is the check list of instructional objectives. This makes it possible to indicate the student's strengths and weaknesses in terms of the specific learning outcomes of the instruction. Since both teaching and evaluation should be based on clearly specified instructional objectives, it seems only logical to follow through and report learning progress on the same basis.

Information Function. Informing parents of their children's achievement and progress in school is a basic function of any marking and reporting system. Parents need such reports if they are to be kept aware of the objectives of the school program and are to cooperate with the school in promoting the learning and development of their children. By knowing their children's successes and failures in schoolwork, parents are better able to provide emotional support, encouragement, and needed guidance to their children.

Reports to parents also serve as a means of maintaining or improving home-school relations. The report form indicates to the parents which aspects of achievement and development the school considers most important. The nature of the report also reflects whether the emphasis is on the positive aspects of learning and development or simply on the student's failures. Many parents have so little contact with the school that the report form becomes a major factor in shaping their attitudes toward the school.

To adequately meet the needs of parents for information concerning the school program and the success of their children in it, a more comprehensive reporting system is needed than that provided by the A, B, C, D, F marking system. As a minimum, check lists of objectives should be provided for parents so that they can note the specific strengths and weaknesses in their students' learning and development. If a parent desires to help his child with arithmetic, for example, it is much more useful to know that the child is having difficulty with multiplication problems than to simply know that he received a letter grade of C in arithmetic.

At the elementary level, the reporting system should include parent-teacher conferences, if at all possible. There is no better way to share information with parents than in a face-to-face conference. This should not replace the more systematic report form, however, but should simply supplement it. The more systematic report form, containing letter grades and check lists of objectives, is needed for reporting to students and for guidance and administrative functions.

Guidance Functions. Reports on student achievement and development can also contribute to more effective guidance and counseling. They can aid in identifying academic areas of strength and weakness and, thus, provide useful information for educational and vocational planning. Reports that include ratings on personal and social characteristics can also be helpful in counseling students with adjustment problems.

Guidance functions demand a more comprehensive report form than that provided by the traditional letter-grade system. Ideally, counselors should participate in the development of the reporting system so that their needs are considered along with those of students, parents, and teachers.

Administrative Functions. The administrative functions served by a marking and reporting system include (1) determining student promotion and graduation, (2) the placement of transfer students, (3) the awarding of scholarships, (4) admission to college, and (5) reporting to prospective employers. For many administrative uses, the traditional letter grade is especially suitable because it is easily recorded and it provides an easily obtained grade point average. The latter is especially useful at the high school level for granting awards and for predicting success in college. It should be noted, also, that practically all colleges require a transcript of letter grades for college admission. Thus, no matter what type of reporting system a school develops, traditional letter grades (or their equivalent) must be retained to satisfy the demands of the colleges.

Some administrative functions are best served by reports that include more than the single letter grade. Decisions concerning student placement, course offerings, curriculum revisions, and the like, can be best made if more comprehensive reports of student achievement are available. Here, it would seem that reports concerning the extent to which the objectives of the school program are being achieved would be especially useful.

The use of pass-fail grades also enters into administrative and curriculum decisions. If pass-fail grading is used in all courses, there will be less information concerning student achievement than that provided by the A, B, C, D, F system. Also, the grade point average will not be available for predicting future school success and for college admission. On the other hand, the limited use of the pass-fail option to encourage students to explore new areas would seem to have a desirable influence on their educational programs, without sacrificing the benefits of the traditional letter-grade system. Typically, courses taken under the pass-fail option are not counted in the student's point average.

In general summary, a multiple marking and reporting system is needed to satisfy the various instructional, information, guidance, and administrative functions in the school. The following methods would seem to be the most useful to include in a comprehensive reporting system.

1. The A, B, C, D, F marking system should be retained for administrative uses and for maintaining permanent school records.
2. Letter grades should be supplemented by checklists of objectives for each subject area and for the areas of personal and social development.
3. Pass-fail grading should be provided as a student option for a limited number of elective courses at the high school and college levels.
4. Parent-teacher conferences should be used at the elementary school level to supplement the more formal report form.

Attempts to replace traditional letter grades (A, B, C, D, F) with other methods of reporting have generally been unsuccessful. Although there may be many reasons for this, there is no question concerning the fact that letter grades are convenient, easily averaged, and serve important administrative functions. Thus, rather than attempting to replace letter grades, efforts should be directed toward *supplementing* them with reports that are more meaningful to students, parents, teachers, and other school personnel. When this is done, the letter grades themselves can be made more meaningful. Rather than being a conglomerate of achievement, effort, attitude, and behavior, letter grades can serve as a pure measure of achievement. The other aspects of student development can be reported on separately in the report.

Factors to Be Included in School Marks and Reports

Although the specific nature of the marking and reporting system can be expected to vary somewhat from one school to another and from one educational level to another, there are some common elements that should be included in the reports. These are (1) achievement, (2) effort, (3) personal and social characteristics, and (4) work habits.

Achievement. The achievement report should indicate the degree to which students are achieving the instructional objectives in each subject area. This achievement should be summarized in a letter grade (A, B, C, D, F) that indicates the student's general level of achievement in the subject area. Each letter grade, however, should be supplemented by a check list of objectives that indicates the student's strengths and weaknesses in learning. This system makes it possible to retain letter grades for school records (for administrative functions) and for reporting to parents (if desired). At the same time, a more diagnostic report of student achievement on each objective is provided for use by students, parents, teachers, and other school personnel.

The letter grades and the check lists of objectives should reflect achievement and achievement only. They should not be contaminated by the teacher's judgment of student effort or student behavior. These elements should be reported on separately. One of the most common criticisms of reporting student learning in terms of single letter grades is that a given grade (e.g., B) is such a conglomerate of diverse elements that only the teacher who gave the grade knows what it means. By limiting letter grades to achievement only and by clarifying them further with reports of student performance on the course objectives, the letter grades become a clearer and more meaningful report of student learning.

Effort. A separate report on student effort will enable the teacher to communicate this information to students and parents without contaminating the achievement grades. All too frequently teachers have used higher grades than are warranted to reward the efforts of low-ability students and used lower grades than are warranted to prod high-ability students into achieving more. This, of course, simply distorts the meaning of the achievement grades.

The report on effort might be in terms of a separate letter grade or it might be included in a check list of objectives or work habits. Because of the importance that students, parents, and teachers attach to effort, a separate letter grade would seem warranted.

Personal and Social Characteristics. Ratings on personal and social characteristics are useful in understanding students and in guiding their personal development. The specific characteristics included on the report form should reflect the objectives of the school program (e.g., Respects the rights of others) as well as the special needs of teachers and counselors. Since the list typically must be kept relatively short (e.g., 6 to 10), to meet the requirements of a compact report form, the characteristics must be very carefully selected. In general, they should be characteristics that are directly observable by teachers and ones that can be stated clearly and concisely. Unless the characteristics are carefully selected and clearly stated, they are not likely to elicit conscientious ratings by teachers.

Work Habits. How a student approaches school tasks provides an insight into his learning and development. Does he start work immediately or does he procrastinate? Does he persist with a task or does he give up easily? Does he complete his work on time or does he typically plod along? These and similar questions need to be considered in developing a check list of relevant work habits. Like the check list of personal and social characteristics, the list of items should be brief and clearly stated.

To summarize, a marking and reporting system should provide separate reports on achievement, effort, personal and social characteristics, and work habits. This will permit the achievement grades to reflect pure achievement and the other reports to supplement and complement the letter grades assigned to each subject area. The specific check lists of objectives for each subject area and for the other characteristics to be rated should be determined by local school personnel in consultation with students and parents. Although the check lists of objectives will vary from one school level to another, to meet the specific needs of different grade levels, the achievement grades (A, B, C, D, F) will provide a continuous and meaningful record of student progress throughout the various grade levels.

Frames of Reference for Judging Student Performance

Student marks and reports are typically based on one of the following frames of reference.

1. Performance relative to the group (Norm referenced).
2. Performance relative to an absolute standard (Criterion referenced).
3. Performance relative to the individual's past achievement or potential.

When student performance is reported in relation to the classroom group, it is called *norm-referenced* marking. In this marking system, the grade a student receives in a particular subject depends on his relative ranking in the group. If he ranks near the top of the group he will receive a letter grade of A. If he ranks lower in the group he will receive a letter grade of B, C, D, or F, depending on his position in the group and the percentage of students assigned each grade. The norm-referenced system does not necessarily mean "marking on the normal curve," and thus assigning an equal number of high and low grades (e.g., 7 per cent As and 7 per cent Fs). It simply means that the grades represent *relative* performance, rather than some absolute level of performance. The percentage of students assigned each grade is typically determined by the school staff, taking into account such factors as the nature of the institution, the student population, the subject area, and the level of instruction. The process of assigning norm-referenced grades is described in the next chapter. Here we are simply clarifying the nature of norm-referenced marking.

When student performance is reported in relation to an absolute standard, it is called *criterion-referenced* marking. With this system, a student's grade is determined by how closely his performance matches the expectations set by the teacher. The teacher's expectations may be defined in terms of specific learning tasks (e.g., typing 40 words per minute with no more than two errors) or in terms of the percentage of learning tasks that the student has mastered. With this system, there is no predetermined distribution of grades. If all students meet the teacher's expectations, all will receive a letter grade of A. Each of the other letter grades is also based on an absolute standard of performance. Where percentage-correct scores are used, letter grades are defined by some percentage-correct range as follows: A (95–100), B (85–94), C (75–84), D (65–74), F (below 65).

Criterion-referenced marking is most useful where the emphasis is on mastery learning. Effective use of absolute standards requires that the learning tasks be well defined, the standards of performance be clearly specified, and the measurement of student performance be criterion referenced (Gronlund, 1973). Only at the mastery learning level are such conditions possible. As typically used in the schools, percentage-correct grades are difficult to interpret because they are based on some unknown conglomerate of learning tasks, on poorly defined standards of performance, and on norm-referenced measurement. Procedures for the proper use of criterion-referenced marking are described in Chapter 4.

Reporting student performance in relation to his own past achievement (i.e., amount of improvement), or his learning potential, poses serious problems for the teacher. Measures of growth over short spans of time are extremely unreliable as are measured differences between learning potential and achievement (Thorndike, 1969). If test results are unreliable in these instances, it is unlikely that teachers' judgments of growth, or learning potential, would be very dependable. Grading on the basis of past achievement or learning potential typically has been used at the elementary school level to motivate low-ability students. If used as a supplement to a mark that indicates level of achievement, it may serve some useful purpose. However, its use should be restricted to such dual marking and its limitations as a measure of achievement should be clearly recognized.

In summary, student performance may be judged in relation to the classroom group (norm referenced), in relation to an absolute standard (criterion referenced), or in relation to the student's own past achievement or learning potential. For most marking and reporting purposes, norm-referenced grading provides the most meaningful system. Where a mastery-learning approach is used, criterion-referenced grading would be a logical extension of the criterion-referenced methods used to measure learning. In some cases, it may be desirable to combine norm-referenced grading and criterion-referenced grading in a dual marking system. One grade could indicate the student's performance in relation to his classmates and the other could indicate the degree to which he had achieved the objectives of the course. Grading in terms of the student's own past achievement or potential should be used sparingly, if at all, and only in conjunction with a more meaningful achievement grade.

Types of Report Forms

The traditional report card includes a place to record a single letter grade (A, B, C, D, F) for each subject and a brief list of characteristics (e.g., work habits) to be rated. As noted earlier, where a single letter grade is used to report student progress it is likely to become a conglomerate measure of achievement, effort, attitude, and behavior. Thus, a letter grade of C may represent above-average achievement that was marked down because of little effort and disciplinary infractions, or it may represent low achievement that was rated higher because of good effort and good behavior. The contamination of letter grades by factors other than achievement are well documented by the research literature (Terwilliger 1966, NEA, 1970).

Newer methods of reporting provide for separate marks or ratings on a number of different aspects of student achievement and development. A sample of such a report form, used at the elementary level, is shown in Figure 1. For each marking period, the student receives a letter grade for achievement (above slanted line), a numerical grade for effort (below slanted line), and a rating on the objectives in each subject area. The bottom portion of the form includes a place for checking those habits and attitudes that are in need of improvement.

Another report form that includes many of the desirable aspects of a multiple-marking system is shown in Figure 2. This form, designed for use at the secondary level, provides for a separate mark on achievement and effort, and for rating on two check lists of objectives. The list of objectives at the

REPORT OF PROGRESS
GRADES 4-5-6
ELEMENTARY SCHOOLS
DISTRICT 194
19_____ 19_____

STUDENT_____

GRADE_____

TEACHER_____

SCHOOL_____

KEY:
A—outstanding
B—above average
C—average
D—below average
F—failing

✔ A check after a statement indicates a need for improvement in that area.
If there are no check marks, the child's progress is satisfactory.

FINAL GRADE		1st GRADE PR.			2nd GRADE PR			3rd GRADE PR.			4th GRADE PR.			COMMENTS
		GOOD	AVG.	POOR	GOOD	AVG.	POOR	GOOD	AVG.	POOR	GOOD	AVG.	POOR	
	READING													
	Understanding													
	Meaning and Word Usage													
	Basic Skills													
	Outside Reading													
	LANGUAGE													
	Oral Expression													
	Written Expression													
	Penmanship													
	SPELLING													
	Basic Words													
	Usage													
	MATHEMATICS													
	Accuracy and Fundamentals													
	Problem Solving													
	SOCIAL STUDIES													
	SCIENCE													
	HEALTH													
	PHYSICAL EDUCATION													
	ART													
	MUSIC													
	Singing Participation													
	Theory													
	CONDUCT													
	HABITS AND ATTITUDES													
	Completes work on time													
	Listens — follows directions													
	Does neat work													
	Contributes to discussions													
	Is courteous and Respectful													
	Has self control													
	Cooperates well													
	Is dependable													
	Is neat in appearance													
	Days absent													
	Days present													
	Fees unpaid													
	Height and weight													

Figure 1. Comprehensive elementary school report form. (Reproduced by permission of School District 194, Steger, Illinois.)

PROGRESS REPORT
University of Illinois High School
Urbana, Illinois

SCIENCE

Science 1   Biology   Chemistry   Physics   Advanced Problems

____ 1st quarter - November   ____ 3rd quarter - April

____ Semester - February   ____ Final Report - June

RATING SCALE: + - Outstanding,   S - Satisfactory,   U - Unsatisfactory,   O - Inadequate basis for judgment.

S U O	Respects rights, opinions and abilities of others	+ S U O Evidences independent thought and originality
S U O	Accepts responsibility for group's progress	+ S U O Seeks more than superficial knowledge
S U O	Is careful with property	+ S U O Shows ability to define problem areas and locate sources of information
S U O	Uses time to advantage	+ S U O Makes accurate and selective interpretation of data
S U O	Is attentive	+ S U O Shows increasing self-direction
S U O	Follows directions	+ S U O Displays mastery of factual information
S U O	Makes regular preparations as required	

ACHIEVEMENT

The grade below is a measure of achievement with respect to what is expected of a pupil of this class in this school, and in relation to what is expected in the next higher course in this subject.

____ 5 excellent   ____ 2 passing, but weak

____ 4 very good   ____ 1 failing

____ 3 creditable   ____ 0 inadequate basis for judgment

EFFORT

The grade below is an estimate, based on evidence available to the teacher, of the individual student's effort.

____ 5 excellent   ____ 2 weak

____ 4 very good   ____ 1 very weak

____ 3 creditable   ____ 0 inadequate basis for judgment

COMMENTS:

Teacher: _____

Figure 2. High school report form illustrating a multiple-marking system. (Reproduced by permission of University High School, Urbana, Illinois.)

upper left contains common school goals that appear on the report forms for all subject areas. The list at the upper right contains those objectives that are unique to a particular subject, in this case science. With this type of report form, it is possible to assign an uncontaminated achievement grade that is useful for administrative functions and at the same time to assign a grade for effort and to inform students and parents of the progress being made toward the common school goals and the course objectives. This form was cooperatively developed by committees of teachers, students, and parents, and thus reflects the type of information they considered most important.

Guidelines for Improving Marking and Reporting

Marking and reporting systems are expected to serve a variety of functions (e.g., instructional, administrative) and are to be used by various persons (e.g., parents, teachers, college admissions officers). Thus, no single, or simple, marking system can be expected to suffice. What is needed is a system that provides some uniformity of reporting for school records and yet can be adapted to local needs and to the special requirements of different grade levels. The following statements are intended to serve as guidelines for developing such a system.

1. **A multiple marking and reporting system should be used.** A letter grade (e.g., A, B, C, D, F) for each subject, representing a pure measure of achievement, should be supplemented by separate reports on course objectives, effort, personal and social characteristics, and work habits. The report should make clear whether the letter grade is norm referenced or criterion referenced. Reports on student performance in terms of improvement or potential, if used at all, should supplement rather than replace the basic achievement grade.

2. **The marking and reporting system should be based on objectives that are clearly stated in measurable terms.** When stated in measurable terms, the same set of objectives can be used for instruction, evaluation, and reporting student progress. The assigned letter grades should reflect the extent to which the instructional objectives in each subject have been achieved. The most important of the instructional objectives for each subject should be added to the report form to further clarify the meaning of the letter grades. Check lists of objectives should also be used for reporting on personal and social characteristics as well as on work habits.

3. **The marking and reporting system should be cooperatively developed by teachers, students, parents, and other school personnel.** To adequately serve the various functions of the reports, it is important that all interested users be involved in developing the marking and reporting system. A committee of interested persons, representing the various groups, should develop a tentative report form that can then be presented to the larger groups for review and revision. It is especially important that the various users of the reports understand the check lists of objectives because these represent the important outcomes of the school program.

4. The report form should be kept as brief and compact as possible. It is desirable to provide as much information as is needed by the users of the report, but this must be balanced off against practical considerations. Preparing the report should not overburden the teachers, and the report should be brief enough that the users will carefully consider all items on it. Too much detail tends to contribute to perfunctory marking and parent misunderstanding.

5. The report form should include only those items on which teachers can be expected to make reasonably valid judgments. Reports of student progress presuppose some type of testing or evaluation. If a particular behavior cannot be directly observed or readily measured by the teacher, it should be omitted from the report form.

6. The report form should encourage two-way communication. It should provide a space for parent comments as well as teacher comments. It might also include a place for the parent to check when a parent-teacher conference is desired.

7. The marking and reporting system should provide for parent-teacher conferences, as needed. At the elementary school level these conferences might be scheduled on a regular basis, but at the high school level they probably should be arranged only at the request of the parent or teacher. Whenever used, parent-teacher conferences should supplement rather than replace the more formal report form.

8. The marking and reporting system should be evaluated in terms of its influence on student learning and development. In the final analysis, the purpose of all educational endeavor is to improve student learning and development. Thus, during the development of the reporting system and during its tryout and use, the over-riding question is "What effect does it have on students?" Does it help them understand their strengths and weaknesses? Does it encourage self-evaluation? Does it motivate and reinforce learning? Does it help parents, teachers, and counselors to understand the students better so that they can be more effective in working with them? Unless the influences are primarily positive, the marking and reporting system should be revised.

In summary, a multiple marking system is needed to meet the varied needs of students, parents, teachers, and other school personnel. With a multiple marking system, the letter grade (A, B, C, D, F) can be retained as a pure measure of achievement, and the other elements of the report form can be designed to meet the special needs of the various users of the reports. The marking and reporting system is most likely to be effective if it is cooperatively developed, is based on the objectives of the school program, and its purpose and nature are clearly conveyed to the users of the reports.

Chapter 3
Assigning Norm-Referenced Letter Grades

The A, B, C, D, F marking system is used in the majority of schools at the elementary, secondary, and college levels. Its use has persisted for more than fifty years, despite frequent attempts to replace it with other marking systems or to abolish school marks altogether. This persistence has probably resulted, at least in part, from the fact that letter grades are easily used, quickly understood, and serve various essential administrative functions (e.g., promotion, college admission). Their widespread and persistent use would seem to indicate that efforts should be directed toward making the letter grades as meaningful as possible and then supplementing them with more detailed reports of student learning and development.

As indicated in Chapter 2, letter grades representing a student's level of achievement may be assigned on a *relative* basis (norm referenced), or in terms of an *absolute* standard of performance (criterion referenced). In this chapter, we describe how to assign norm-referenced letter grades. Criterion-referenced marking and reporting are considered in the following chapter.

The effective use of letter grades in school marking involves a number of specific considerations, such as the following:

1. How can we obtain letter grades that are valid indicators of achievement?
2. How should the various types of achievement data be combined in assigning grades?
3. What distribution of letter grades should be used?
4. On what basis should promotion and retention be decided?
5. How should letter grades be supplemented for more comprehensive reporting?

Each of these issues is discussed in relation to the assignment of A, B, C, D, F grades on a relative (norm-referenced) basis.

Letter Grades As Valid Indicators of Achievement

Letter grades are likely to be most meaningful and useful when they represent a pure measure of achievement. This means that they should reflect the extent to which students have achieved the learning outcomes of the course and should not be contaminated by effort, personal behavior, and other extraneous factors. This also means that the grades must be based on accurate and valid measures of student learning. Letter grades cannot serve as valid indicators of achievement unless the measurement and evaluation results on which they are based are also valid.

Informal classroom tests play a major role in assigning letter grades in most areas of study. To ensure valid results, the tests should be designed to measure all important outcomes of the instruction and not just those that are easy to measure. A common procedure for constructing classroom tests with good content validity is to follow these steps:

1. State the instructional objectives in measurable terms.
2. Outline the content of instruction.
3. Build a table of specifications that indicates the emphasis to be given to each objective and each area of content.
4. Construct test items to fit the specifications.

These steps provide greater assurance that the various learning outcomes, from simple to complex, will be measured in a balanced manner (Gronlund, 1971).

Some learning outcomes cannot be adequately measured by paper-and-pencil tests. Performance skills such as typing, giving a speech, or doing an experiment, require some kind of procedure or product evaluation. To obtain more accurate judgments, such evaluation should be guided by a rating scale, check list, or at least a clearly specified set of criteria for making the judgments. In evaluating written reports (e.g., themes, term papers, laboratory reports), special efforts should be made to prevent such factors as neatness, spelling, and length from unduly influencing the results. In short, we can enhance the validity of our grading by making our evaluations of student performance as directly relevant and as objective as possible.

Where attitude, interest, and other affective outcomes are considered to be important objectives of a course, it would be desirable to evaluate and report on these separately, rather than incorporate them in the achievement grade. If the intended outcomes of a course are primarily affective (e.g., appreciation of music), it may be desirable to use a pass-fail or satisfactory-unsatisfactory grade and not include these grades in the grade-point average.

Combining Data in Assigning Grades

Final course grades are typically based on various types of student achievement, such as short quizzes, term projects, laboratory work, and examinations. Thus, assigning course grades involves combining these various measures into a composite score in such a way that each element receives its intended weight. If we decide, for example, that the final examination should count twice as much as the short quizzes, we then want to make certain that our grades reflect this emphasis. Similarly, if we decide that laboratory work should make up 25 per cent of the final course grade, we want some assurance that it will be represented to that extent. It is not uncommon for teachers to communicate to students what elements will be included in the final grade and the relative weight to be assigned to each.

Determining how much weight should be given to each of the various types of achievement is a matter of judgment. This judgment is guided by the importance of the various instructional objectives, the teaching emphasis given to each type of course activity, the reliability and validity of the measures used, and similar considerations. In some cases, the teachers in a particular department might agree on the composition of final grades in each course. More often, the individual teacher must decide on the relative emphasis to be allocated.

When the decision has been made concerning what proportion of the weight is to be allocated to each measure of student performance, the measures must be combined in such a way that the desired weighting is obtained. To illustrate the problems in the weighting of achievement data, let us use a simple example. Assume that we want to combine scores on an examination and scores on a term project, and that we want them to contribute equally to the final grade. Our scores on the two measures are as follows:

Range of scores on examination	20 to 120
Range of scores on term project	40 to 60

If we simply add together the examination score and the project score for each individual, the final grade will be determined largely by how well the students' performed on the examination. To illustrate this, let us compare a student who is highest on the examination and lowest on the term project (Student A) with a student who is highest on the term project and lowest on the examination (Student B).

	Student A	Student B
Examination score	120	20
Term project score	40	60
Composite score	160	80

It is obvious that simply adding the two scores will not give them equal representation in the composite score. The examination score has much greater influence than the term project score.

In a situation such as this, teachers frequently attempt to equate the influence of the two measures by making the maximum possible score equivalent. In our example, this would mean multiplying the student's term project score by two, to make the total possible score 120 for both measures of achievement. Let us see how our two hypothetical students would fare under this system.

	Student A	Student B
Examination score	120	20
Term project score (x 2)	80	120
Composite score	200	140

It is obvious that equating on the basis of maximum possible score does not provide for equal emphasis in the composite score either. The examination score still has the greater influence when the two are combined. This is so because the contribution a given measure makes to a composite score depends largely on the variability, or spread, of the scores in the set.

To give our two measures equal weight in the composite score, we would need to examine the range of scores for each and to adjust our scores accordingly. Since our examination scores have a range of 100 (120 − 20) and our term project scores a range of 20 (60 − 40), we would need to multiply each term project score by 5 to obtain equal weight. Let us check our two hypothetical students using this procedure.

	Student A	Student B
Examination score	120	20
Term project score (x 5)	200	300
Composite score	320	320

Our check shows that the multiplication factor of 5, based on the range of scores, gives the two measures equal weight in the composite score. If we wanted our term project scores to count *twice* as much as our examination scores, we would, of course, have to multiply each term project score by 10.

The range of scores provides a fairly good approximation for determining the multiplication factor(s) to use in weighting components of a composite score for grading purposes. More refined weighting can be obtained by using the standard deviation, but the additional computation required tends to discourage its use for routine classroom grading. A description of how to use the standard deviation in determining composite scores can be obtained in a book on grading by Terwilliger (1971).

Some teachers prefer to combine data from various sources by converting all scores to letter grades (A, B, C, D, F) and then averaging the letter grades to determine the final mark. When this is done, information is lost. For example, a student with the highest B and a high A would receive the same average grade as a student with the lowest B and a low A. Averaging the scores before converting to letter grades would most likely result in an A for the first student and a B for the second. Thus, for most grading purposes it would seem desirable to average raw scores and to obtain the desired weighting by using the range of scores as previously described. Where it is necessary to average letter grades, the use of pluses and minuses on the letter grades will reduce the loss of information and increase the accuracy of the results.

Determining the Distribution of Grades

When various measures of achievement have been combined into a composite score for each student in a classroom group, we can then rank the students from high to low in terms of overall achievement. Our next step is to assign a letter grade to each student. Before this can be done, however, it is necessary to make a decision concerning the number of As, Bs, Cs, Ds, and Fs to be assigned. This is no simple decision, and it may be resolved in different ways.

Grading on the Normal Curve. One common practice in grading has been to assign grades on the basis of the normal curve. This practice, which was first introduced in 1908 (Cureton, 1971), assumes that student achievement is normally distributed and, therefore, grading on the normal curve is appropriate.

The normal curve is illustrated in Figure 3, with a typical normal distribution of grades indicated along the base line. It will be noted that with this system the largest proportion of students receive C grades and the percentage of A and B grades are matched by an equivalent percentage of F and D grades. Thus, no matter how good the group is, a fixed percentage will receive Fs; or, conversely, no matter how poor the group is, a fixed percentage will receive As. With grading on the normal curve, the percentage of students receiving each grade is predetermined and the number of high grades are balanced by an equivalent number of low grades.

Although grading on the curve seems to provide an objective method for assigning grades, the assumption that student achievement is normally distributed is seldom warranted with classroom groups. As Terwilliger (1971) has pointed out, the size of the groups is typically too small to expect a normal distribution, and teachers' measures of student achievement seldom yield normally distributed scores. In addition, the student population becomes increasingly more select as it moves through the high school and college levels

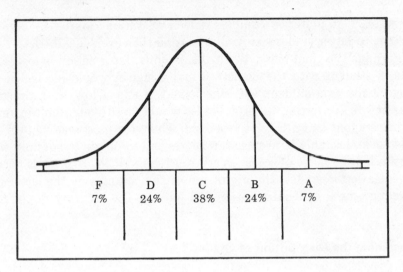

Figure 3.   Normal curve with a typical distribution of grades.

since the less able students either fail or drop out of school. It is educationally unsound to continue to give the same proportion of F grades in these more select student populations.

Setting an Appropriate Distribution of Grades. The approximate distribution of letter grades should be set by the school staff, taking into account the nature of the course, the type of student population, and the purposes to be served by the grades. An introductory course, for example, might have the following suggested distribution of grades:

A — 10 to 20 per cent
B — 20 to 30 per cent
C — 40 to 50 per cent
D — 10 to 20 per cent
F — 0 to 10 per cent

Such a distribution provides clear guidelines for the individual teacher to follow and yet provides for some flexibility in assigning grades. Thus, the teacher can scan a list of composite scores and look for natural breaks in assigning grades. The range for each letter grade also makes it possible for the teacher to adjust for an especially good, or especially poor, class.

Separate suggested grade distributions might be determined for introductory and advanced courses. Similarly, special distributions might be specified for gifted and slow learning classes. The nature of the grade distributions should be developed by local school personnel and clearly communicated to all teachers and to all users of the reports. It is impossible to obtain a standard meaning for letter grades from one school system to another, but at least within a given school system there should be some uniform policy for assigning grades; this policy should be made explicit to all concerned.

Deciding Promotion and Retention. It will be noted in our suggested distribution of grades that the proportion of students to be given the grade of F ranges from 0 to 10 per cent. This latitude is important since failure in a course should be determined by more than a student's *relative* position in the group. The important question is, "Does this student have a good enough command of the minimum essentials of the subject to succeed at the next highest level of instruction?" If he does he should pass; if he doesn't he probably should fail. Thus, even when we are assigning letter grades on a relative (normative) basis, the pass-fail decision must be made on an absolute (criterion-referenced) basis.

Terwilliger (1971) suggests that the pass-fail decision be based on a mastery test of the minimal objectives of the course, with a passing standard set at 80 to 90 per cent correct. Although a test of this type would be useful in making this decision, other types of achievement (e.g., performance skills, laboratory work, and so on) should, of course, also be considered. Elementary teachers might also want to take into consideration factors other than achievement in deciding promotion. For example, a socially immature student, who is borderline in achievement, might be held back if the teacher feels that his total development would be best provided for in his present grade.

In summary, the normal curve provides an inappropriate basis for assigning grades because the assumption of a normal distribution of student achievement is seldom valid. The approximate distributions of letter grades should be determined by the school staff, and individual teachers should be expected to stay within the agreed upon guidelines. Although normative letter grades are assigned on a relative basis, the pass-fail decision should be based on whether the student has achieved the minimum skills needed to succeed at the next level of instruction.

Supplementing Norm-Referenced Letter Grades

Some school marking and reporting systems consist of a single letter grade in each subject. This may be satisfactory at the college level, where grades are used primarily for administrative decisions (e.g., graduation, certification). At the elementary and secondary levels, however, it would be desirable to provide a more comprehensive report of student learning. The two most common methods of supplementing norm-referenced letter grades are the use of dual marking and the use of checklists of instructional objectives.

Dual Marking. Several types of dual marking systems can be used with relative (norm-referenced) grading. Some of the more common combinations are the following:

1. Relative achievement — Absolute achievement
2. Relative achievement — Achievement in respect to potential

3. Relative achievement — Growth in achievement
4. Relative achievement — Effort

The type of dual marking system to be used depends largely on the purposes to be served by the reports. Letter grades indicating relative achievement will adequately serve the school's administrative functions. Thus, the second mark in the dual system should be selected in terms of its contribution to the other functions served by marks (e.g., instruction, guidance, reports to parents). An example of a report form using a dual marking system is presented in Figure 2, Chapter 2.

Check Lists of Objectives. As indicated earlier, various aspects of achievement are combined in assigning letter grades in school subjects. Thus, although the single letter grade might be confined to achievement only, it is still a conglomerate of different types of achievement. From an instructional standpoint, there is considerable advantage in reporting on each of the several aspects of achievement separately. This is typically done by listing the most important instructional objectives for each course and reporting on these, in addition to assigning a composite achievement grade. The report forms in Figures 1 and 2, Chapter 2, illustrate the use of supplementary check lists of objectives.

In general, summary, norm-referenced letter grades provide a simple and convenient indicator of student achievement. To be most effective, they should represent pure achievement, they should be based on valid evaluation data, and the approximate distribution of grades should be agreed upon by the school staff. The pass-fail decision should be typically based on whether the student has achieved the minimum objectives of the course rather than simply on his relative position in the group. Although single letter grades serve the administrative functions of the school well, they are inadequate for meeting the instructional, guidance, and information functions of an effective reporting system. Thus, wherever possible, norm-referenced letter grades should be supplemented by more comprehensive reports of student learning and development. Dual marking and check lists of objectives provide a convenient method of doing this.

Chapter 4
Criterion-Referenced Marking and Reporting

Criterion-referenced marking and reporting involves judging student performance in terms of specified performance standards. We might, for example, describe expected student performance with statements such as the following:

> Multiplies all combinations of single-digit whole numbers without error.
> Defines 85 per cent of the technical terms in the instructional unit.
> Types 40 words per minute with no more than two errors.

Statements such as these make clear the precise nature of the expected student performance and the level of proficiency that is desired. Thus, such statements provide an absolute standard for judging student achievement. There is no need to compare a student's achievement to the other members of the classroom group. If he can demonstrate the degree of competence that has been specified for a set of learning tasks, his achievement is satisfactory regardless of the level of performance of his classmates.

At first glance, this appears to be a simple and sensible way to judge and report student achievement. There are numerous problems involved in using this approach, however, and most of them can be dealt with in only an approximate manner. Some of the more obvious problems are as follows:

1. **The problem of delimiting and defining the domain of learning tasks to be achieved by students.** In highly structured subjects, such as mathematics, the domain of learning outcomes can be clearly delimited, the learning tasks can be precisely stated, and the instructional units can be arranged in a sequential, or hierarchical, order. This makes it possible to report student achievement in terms of a hierarchically structured set of clearly defined learning tasks. In arithmetic, for example, we might report that a student can solve 90 per cent of the three-digit addition problems that involve no carrying, but only 60 per cent of problems that require simply carrying and 20 per cent of the problems that require repeated carrying. Such a report is meaningful because of the natural structure of the subject.

In loosely structured subjects, such as social studies, the domain of learning tasks is difficult to delmiit and define, and there is no clear hierarchical structure. The content and sequential order of topics in social studies can be expected to vary widely from one teacher to another. This, of course, provides a poor frame of reference for judging and reporting student performance in terms of an absolute standard.

2. **The problem of stating the instructional objectives in performance terms.** If student achievement is to be reported in terms of level of performance on a particular set of learning tasks, the behavior involved in the performance must be clearly defined. This is done by stating the instructional objectives in terms of the types of behavior students are expected to demonstrate when they have achieved the intended learning outcomes. The several statements at the beginning of this chapter illustrate instructional objectives of this type.

The problem involved here is that some instructional objectives are easy to define in performance terms whereas others are not. In general, simple learning outcomes (e.g., defines terms) are more easily defined than complex ones (e.g., applies principles), and some outcomes are so difficult to define (e.g., appreciation) that they are likely to be completely neglected. Thus, with criterion-referenced reporting there is always the danger that lower level outcomes will be overemphasized.

3. **The problem of setting appropriate standards of student performance.** A major problem in using criterion-referenced marking and reporting is that of specifying meaningful standards of performance. If the report is in terms of instructional objectives, a judgment must be made concerning what level of knowledge or skill is needed to demonstrate satisfactory achievement on each objective. If the report is in terms of letter grades (A, B, C, D, F), a judgment must be made concerning what levels of proficiency are to be encompassed by each letter grade. These are judgments that must be made by the teacher, with relatively few helpful guidelines to follow. A common procedure is to use percentage-correct scores (e.g., spells 90 per cent of the words, or A = 90–100), but the particular percentage used is typically determined in an arbitrary manner.

4. **The problem of obtaining criterion-referenced measures of student performance.** Criterion-referenced marking and reporting is most effective when student achievement is measured with criterion-referenced instruments; that is, with tests and evaluation devices that are designed to yield descriptions of student performance in absolute terms. Measuring instruments that are designed to simply rank students in order of achievement (e.g., norm-referenced tests) seldom provide adequate descriptions of student performance. Thus, they make absolute judgments of performance extremely difficult, if not impossible.

Criterion-referenced measurement requires a delimited domain of learning tasks that is clearly defined in terms of student performance. This is typically done by (1) dividing the instruction into relatively small units (a week or two), (2) specifying the learning outcomes for each unit in performance terms, and (3) measuring all of the intended outcomes of the unit, or a representative sample of them (Gronlund, 1973). As noted earlier, the process of dividing instruction into meaningful segments, and of clearly defining the learning tasks in each segment, is easier in some subjects (e.g., mathematics) than in others (e.g., social studies) and is easier for some types of learning (e.g., simple skills) than for others (e.g., complex outcomes). Thus, where criterion-referenced marking and reporting is adopted, it will require more systematic testing and evaluation than is typically done by classroom teachers, and it will pose special problems for teachers in some areas of instruction.

At present, criterion-referenced marking and reporting is most useful where group instruction is based on a mastery-learning approach (e.g., Bloom's mastery-learning approach) or where the instruction has been completely individualized (Gronlund, 1974). Both teaching methods require dividing the instruction into clearly defined learning units, specifying the objectives in performance terms, and using criterion-referenced measures to determine student achievement. In the case of individualized instruction, criterion-referenced marking and reporting is essential since students work on different units at different times and frequently are not expected to complete a common set of units (Gronlund, 1974). Marking on a relative basis is inappropriate where each student is working on his own individual program of study.

Before examining the role of criterion-referenced marking and reporting in mastery learning and individualized instruction, let us first examine the conventional use of absolute standards in grading.

Conventional Grading with Absolute Standards

A survey of 129 secondary schools by Terwilliger (1971) revealed that 27 per cent of the teachers used an absolute standard of achievement in determining student grades. Whether this is typical of secondary school teachers throughout the country cannot be determined, but it nonetheless indicates that some teachers favor grading on an absolute basis.

Conventional grading on the basis of absolute standards typically involves the use of percentage-correct scores. These scores are either used directly in reporting or, to define the categories in a letter-grade system. Thus, a set of letter grades might be defined as follows:

A = 95–100
B = 85–94
C = 75–84
D = 65–74
F = below 65

The range of percentage-correct scores can be expected to vary slightly from one school to another, but the basic grading procedure is the same.

In most cases, teachers who grade on an absolute basis lack an adequate frame of reference for making such judgments. They typically do not have a clearly defined domain of learning tasks that delimits and prescribes, in specific behavioral terms, the types of performance students are expected to demonstrate at different levels of achievement. Nor do they often use criterion-referenced measuring instruments for judging student achievement on an absolute basis. All too frequently, absolute grading is based on norm-referenced tests that have been constructed to yield scores that fall some-where between 60 and 100 per cent correct. If the test turns out to be too difficult for the group, some type of adjustment is made. As Millman (1970) has indicated, "these adjustments take such forms as giving another test, raising marks by some mysterious formula, making the next test easier, and altering grading standards." In any event, such grades typically reflect ad-justed percentage-correct scores on some poorly defined hodgepodge of learning tasks.

Assigning letter grades on the basis of an absolute standard is defensible only where a criterion-referenced system of measurement and evaluation is uti-lized. Such a system implies, of course, that the domain of learning tasks, the instructional objectives, and the standards of performance are all clearly spe-cified (Gronlund, 1973). Unless the frame of reference is well defined, grades based on absolute standards are difficult to interpret in a meaningful manner.

Criterion-Referenced Reporting and Mastery Learning

Grading on the basis of absolute standards of achievement is most effective where mastery learning is being emphasized. This is so because the necessary conditions for a criterion-referenced system (e.g., clearly specified sets of learning tasks) can be more easily met, and the percentage-correct score pro-vides a meaningful report. Where mastery is the goal, the percentage-correct score provides a reasonable indicator of the degree to which a student's per-formance is approaching complete mastery.

As Williams and Miller (1973) have noted, there are two methods of assign-ing letter grades in a criterion-referenced system. The first is the "one-shot" method, where the standards are established and the student is assigned a letter grade on the basis of how well he performs on his first attempt to achieve the prespecified standards. The second method is the one used in Bloom's mastery-learning approach (Gronlund, 1974). With this method, if the student fails to achieve a specified level of mastery on a unit of work, he is free to use additional learning time and special corrective techniques until a satisfactory level of mastery is achieved. Thus, the first method is likely to result in some failures, whereas the second method provides a means by which all students can attain success.

With a mastery-learning approach, such as Bloom's, course grades are typically based on the students' final level of achievement. This may be a comprehensive examination over all units of course work or some other appropriate measure. The standards for each letter grade are typically prespecified in terms of percentage-correct scores and are closely followed. For example, if all students achieve the level of mastery specified for an A grade, all will receive A grades. No attempt is made to obtain some predetermined proportion of As, Bs, and Cs. Each grade is assigned on the basis of the level of mastery specified for it.

In some schools where a mastery-learning approach is used, letter grades are replaced (or supplemented) by progress reports showing which instructional objectives each student has mastered. A typical report form used for this type of reporting is shown in Figure 4. There is, of course, a separate report form like this one for each school subject. Each form has a pink, yellow, and green carbon copy attached to it, so four copies of each report are obtained from a single marking.

When this report form was first used, teachers were instructed to simply check the objectives that each student *had acquired* and *had not acquired* by the end of each marking period. This later was changed to assigning a numerical rating for each objective as follows:

HAS ACQUIRED

1 - skill well developed,
   good proficiency
2 - skill developed satisfactorily,
   proficiency could be improved
3 - *basic* skill developed,
   low proficiency,
   needs additional work

NOT ACQUIRED

4 - *basic* skill *not* acquired

This numerical rating of student progress is intended to provide a more complete report than that provided by the simple *mastery-nonmastery* method of reporting.

Reporting in terms of student mastery on each instructional objective requires that a reasonable level of mastery be set for each objective. On mastery tests, the criterion for mastery is commonly set somewhere between 80 and 90 per cent correct. The specific percentage depends on such factors as the nature of the objective being measured, the type of test used, and the level of mastery needed to learn effectively at the next stage of instruction (Gronlund, 1973). On objectives related to some skills (e.g., typing, measurement), standards of mastery can be set in terms of physical measurement; for example,

ROSELLE SCHOOL DISTRICT NO. 12
ROSELLE JUNIOR HIGH SCHOOL

PROGRESS REPORT TO PARENTS 19____ – 19____

Pupil_____   **Language Arts**   Teacher_____

Basic Skills – Blank indicates skill not covered or evaluated

	HAS ACQUIRED	NOT ACQUIRED

1. Ability to infer the main idea of a selection
2. Ability to identify the main parts of a story
3. Ability to draw comparisons
4. Ability to find specific details and imagery
5. Ability to use vocabulary skills
6. Ability to write proper sentences, paragraphs
7. Ability to punctuate
8. Spelling skills
9. Oral reading
10. Library skills

Social Growth, Work Habits, Attitudes

+ indicates strength
Blank indicates acceptable development
– indicates need for improvement

1. Self-discipline
2. Acceptance of responsibility
3. Positive attitude toward authority
4. Class participation
5. Independence in doing assignments
6. Completion of assignments
7. Positive influence in class
8. Positive effort
9. School work affected by frequent absences
    (√) if applicable

If a parent desires a conference, call the school for an appointment – 529-1600

Figure 4.   Report form used with a mastery learning approach. (Reproduced by permission of Roselle School District No. 12, Roselle, Illinois.)

the speed of a performance (e.g., type 40 words per minute) or the precision with which a task is performed (e.g., measure length within one-sixteenth of an inch).

Criterion-Referenced Reporting and Individualized Instruction

Individualized instruction is also based on the concept of mastery learning but it differs considerably from the use of mastery learning in a traditional classroom setting. In the traditional setting, a majority of the learning experiences are group oriented and students work on common learning tasks much of the time. Additional study time, with remedial aid, is provided only for those students who fail to achieve mastery within the group setting. Thus, adjustments in individual programs of study are used primarily as a supplement to group instruction for those students who need it. Programs of individualized instruction, on the other hand, typically permit each student to work on a series of individual study units at his own pace and his own level of learning. In some programs, the instructional units are prescribed by the teacher; whereas in others, students are given considerable freedom in choosing the instructional units that make up their individual programs of study (Gronlund, 1974).

The instructional units used in individualized instruction typically include (1) one or more behaviorally stated objectives, (2) a pretest to measure entry behavior, (3) a specified set of materials and learning activities for achieving the objectives, (4) a self-test to aid the student in monitoring his own learning, and (5) a posttest for measuring terminal achievement. The tests are criterion-referenced, and mastery of the unit is demonstrated by achieving a specified standard (e.g., 85 per cent correct) on the posttest. Thus, students work through a program of study unit-by-unit, demonstrating mastery on each unit before proceeding to the next one.

In programs where students are expected to work through a common set of instructional units, but at their own pace, a convenient report form is one that simply lists the instructional units and provides a place to record the date that each unit is completed by the student. A report form of this type is shown in Figure 5. Using a goal card such as this, in each subject, provides a continuous and detailed report of each student's learning progress.

In programs where students have some choice in the units they will study, the common set of instructional units that are to be studied by all students can be listed at the top of the goal card and the remainder of the card can be left blank. As each student plans his individual program of study for a subject, the optional units selected for study can be added to the card. In this way, the goal card provides a convenient form for recording a student's unique program of study in each subject and for periodically reporting on his learning progress.

Winnetka Public Schools

MATHEMATICS GOAL RECORD CARD 7-8

Pupil_____ Teacher_____ Year_____

REVIEW:	Fall Score	Spring Score
Test 1 – NUMERATION	_____	_____
2 – SETS	_____	_____
3 – ADD. & SUBT. OF WHOLE NUMBERS	_____	_____
4 – MULT. & DIV. OF WHOLE NUMBERS	_____	_____
5 – NUMBER THEORY	_____	_____
6 – MEANING OF FRACTIONAL NUMBERS	_____	_____
7 – ADD. & SUBT. OF FRACTIONAL NUMBERS	_____	_____
8 – MULT. & DIV. OF FRACTIONAL NUMBERS	_____	_____
9 – MEANING OF DECIMAL FRACTIONS	_____	_____
10 – OPERATIONS WITH DECIMAL FRACTIONS	_____	_____

GOALS: Date

I – NUMERATION . . . .   _____
   a) Billions . . . . (   )
   b) Exponent Form . . . . ( )

II – WHOLE NUMBERS . . . .   _____
   a) Addition and Subtraction . . . . ( )
   b) Multiplication . . . . ( )
   c) Division . . . . ( )
   d) Meaning of Properties . . . . ( )

III – NUMBER SENTENCES . . . .   _____

IV – PRIMES AND FACTORS . . . .   _____

V – FRACTIONAL NUMBERS – COMMON . . . .   _____
   a) Meaning . . . . ( )
   b) Addition and Subtraction . . . . ( )
   c) Multiplication and Division . . . . ( )

VI – DECIMALS . . . .   _____
   a) Meaning . . . . ( )
   b) Addition and Subtraction . . . . ( )
   c) Multiplication and Division . . . . ( )

VII – GEOMETRY – NON-METRIC . . . .   _____
   a) Point, Line, Line Segment . . . . ( )
   b) Plane Figures . . . . ( )
   c) Rays and Angles . . . . ( )

VIII – RATIO AND PROPORTION . . . .   _____

IX – PERCENTAGE . . . .   _____
   a) Meaning . . . . ( )
   b) Problem Solving . . . . ( )

X – GEOMETRY – METRIC . . . .   _____
   a) Perimeter . . . . ( )
   b) Area . . . . ( )

Figure 5. Goal card for reporting individual progress. (Reproduced by permission of Winnetka Public Schools, Winnetka, Illinois.)

Some national programs of individualized instruction (e.g., PLAN*) periodically provide teachers with computer-generated reports of learning progress for each student (Gronlund, 1974). These reports show in detail the work that has been completed. Such reports can be used directly in conferences with students and parents, or the information can be summarized on a standard report form such as the goal card.

Letter grades are typically not recommended for use with programs of individualized instruction. Since students work at different rates, frequently do not study instructional units in the same sequence, and may even study different sets of instructional units, there is seldom a common standard by which their performance can be judged. The list of units that has been mastered by each student provides the most meaningful report of individualized learning progress.

Chapter 5
Parent-Teacher Conferences

The parent-teacher conference is widely used for reporting student progress at the elementary level and is used for dealing with special problem situations at the secondary level. As noted in Chapter 1, it is a flexible procedure that permits two-way communication, allows for extensive reporting and sharing of information, and provides teachers and parents with an opportunity to cooperatively develop plans for assisting students with their learning and development. The face-to-face conference also provides the best setting for airing grievances, overcoming misunderstandings, and dealing with special problems concerning a student's learning progress.

Using the conference method for reporting to parents on a regular basis is very time consuming. Each conference typically takes from fifteen to thirty minutes, and additional time is, of course, required to prepare for each conference. A common procedure is to have both fall and spring conferences with parents. Ideally, the fall conferences are scheduled late enough to give the teachers time to know the students and to obtain measures of learning progress (e.g., November), and the spring conferences are scheduled early enough (e.g., March) to permit the results to be used effectively. During the conference sessions, teachers are typically relieved of their teaching responsibilities by using substitutes or by dismissing their classes.

Conferences with parents are likely to be most effective where the teacher plans carefully and where the conference is conducted in accord with sound conference techniques. Guidelines for this purpose are presented in the following sections. It is not expected that knowledge, alone, will result in needed conference skills, however. Teachers who are inexperienced in conducting interviews with parents should be provided with in-service training, including some role playing of typical parent-teacher conferences. Assuming the role of a parent can provide insight into the parent's feelings, and assuming the role of the teacher provides practice in the use of conference skills.

Preparing for the Conference

Most teachers feel uneasy about meeting parents in a conference situation. They want to make a good impression on the parents and they are somewhat fearful that conference situations will arise that they cannot handle. In-service training and role playing can alleviate some of this uneasiness. Careful preparation for the conference is also a good antidote for such apprehension. The following guidelines should be helpful in this regard.

1. **Have a clear grasp of the purpose of the conference.** Reporting student progress to parents in a conference setting involves giving an accurate description of the student's learning progress, obtaining information from the parents, answering any questions the parents might have about the school program, and planning with the parents the most effective means for promoting the student's learning and development. Thus, it is a sharing of information that focuses on the student's strengths and weaknesses and on positive steps that can be taken at home and school to assist the student.

2. **Review the student's school records for general background information.** Knowledge of a student's measured learning ability, past achievement, and adjustment to school is useful in interpreting his present learning progress. If possible, the student's cumulative record should not only be reviewed but should be taken to the conference. Typically, the record is not shown to parents but it may be necessary to refer to it in answering questions.

3. **Assemble a folder of specific information concerning the student's present learning progress.** This should include sample tests, various examples of the student's work, anecdotal descriptions of his behavior, and any other specific information that will contribute to a better understanding of the student's learning progress. Showing a spelling test to a parent is much more effective than simply saying the student is "weak in spelling." Also, specific examples of the student's classroom work help shift the emphasis from *judging* student shortcomings to talking about those skills that need improvement.

4. **Organize the information to be presented to parents in a systematic manner.** Some schools provide a guide sheet that outlines the conference procedure. (See sample guide in Appendix B.) If a check list of objectives (such as those shown in Chapter 4) is used for reporting student progress, the conference materials can be organized to fit the order on the written report form. In any event, having materials ready and well organized will avoid embarrassing moments and will save precious conference time.

5. **Make a tentative list of questions to ask the parents.** These should be questions about the student's attitude toward schoolwork, his interests and hobbies, and similar things that might help clarify the student's total development. Personal questions that are likely to be embarrassing to the parents should, of course, be avoided.

6. **Anticipate parent's questions.** Some schools ask parents to list the things they want to talk about on the parent appointment slip. Whether or not this is done, the teacher can expect parents to ask questions about their

children's learning and development, and about the school program. It is helpful to mentally review the types of questions that parents are likely to ask and to think of appropriate answers. This process may result in further scrutiny of the student's record and another look at school policy. Although a teacher is not expected to be able to answer all questions that parents ask, some thoughtful consideration beforehand will increase the number of questions that can be effectively answered.

7. Provide a comfortable informal setting that is free from interruption. This is difficult to fully achieve since it is frequently necessary to hold the conference in the regular classroom. However, there are some positive steps that can be taken. Provide large enough chairs for the parents to sit on and arrange the chairs so that you won't be sitting behind the desk. An informal arrangement creates a better atmosphere for sharing information with parents on an equal basis. The classroom itself should, of course, be neat and orderly, but students' work might be on display around the room. If the conference is held elsewhere (e.g., the teachers' lounge), take every precaution to keep it free from interruptions.

Conducting the Conference

Successful use of the conference method for reporting student progress to parents involves giving special attention to the following basic phases of the conference.

1. Establishing and maintaining rapport with parents.
2. Sharing information with parents.
3. Planning a course of action with parents.

Guidelines for conducting the parent-teacher conference are presented for each of these phases, in turn.

Establishing and Maintaining Rapport. Good rapport refers to a relationship between two people that is marked by cooperation, harmony, and accord. This is the type of relationship that is needed between parents and teacher to make the conference most effective. Guidelines for establishing rapport with parents include the following.

1. Create a friendly informal atmosphere. The correspondence with parents arranging for the conference should set the tone for the meeting. It should be friendly and informal and stress the importance of cooperative action in aiding the student to achieve maximum educational growth. When the parents arrive for the conference they should be greeted with a smile and a friendly comment. From this beginning, every attempt should be made to create a relaxed and unhurried atmosphere. The focus of attention, however, should be directed toward the main purpose of the meeting. Establishing rapport is one thing, but letting the conference drift off into a social visit is quite another.

2. **Maintain a positive attitude.** Developing a cooperative and harmonious relationship with parents requires that a positive attitude be maintained throughout the conference. Parents are especially sensitive to criticism of their children's accomplishments and behavior and are easily put on the defensive. The judicious use of praise and recognition in discussing the student's strengths and an approach to the student's weaknesses from the point of view, that "here are some areas needing improvement" will go a long way toward maintaining rapport with parents.

3. **Use language that is understandable to parents.** Good rapport depends in part on effective communication. Thus, avoid the use of educational terms and phrases that are not likely to be fully understood by parents. For example, it would be better to talk about a student's "ability to learn" than about his "scholastic aptitude." Using language that is natural to parents has a dual benefit. It enhances teacher-parent communication and it helps to put the parents at ease.

4. **Be willing to listen to parents.** Some parents will express themselves freely, whereas others will need to be encouraged to talk. In either case, they should have the opportunity to provide suggestions, to ask questions, and to voice any criticism they may have concerning the school program. In some cases, it is difficult to proceed with the conference until a parent has had a chance to express himself on some issue that has been bothering him. Listening attentively and accepting his feelings and attitudes, without approving or disapproving of them, will help the parent get it off his chest. In such a situation, it is important not to become argumentative. Simply listening, or reflecting the parent's feelings (e.g., "You feel that school marks are unfair to some students?"), will help the parent express his concerns and reduce the accompanying tension. As his emotion subsides, explanations can be given, if appropriate, or attention can be redirected to the main purpose of the conference.

5. **Be honest and sincere with parents and do not betray confidences.** It is important to be tactful and positive with parents, but if there is a problem it should be discussed with them. Do not attempt to cover up the problem or diminish its importance. Parents will appreciate a frank discussion as long as it is approached with a sincere interest in helping the child. In such discussions, however, any information a child has given in confidence should not be told to the parents without the child's consent. Similarly, any confidential information obtained from parents must be so honored. Mutual trust and confidence are basic ingredients for developing and maintaining effective relations with both students and parents.

Sharing Information with Parents. The sharing of information with parents during the conference can follow different patterns, but the following guidelines outline an effective procedure.

1. **Begin by describing the student's strong points.** The teacher should probably talk first since the parents are eager to hear how their child is doing in school. Beginning with positive comments about the student's strengths tends to ease the parents' apprehension and makes it easier for them to

objectively consider the child's weak points. Enumerating the child's strong points also provides the parents with positive information that they can use when the child asks, "What did the teacher say about me?" In addition to describing the student's strong points, specific examples of his work should be shown to the parents.

2. **Describe the areas needing improvement in a positive and tactful manner.** Be specific in presenting areas in which improvement is needed. Show examples of the student's work and describe the steps you are taking to help the student improve his learning and development. In some instances, it might be desirable to explain why you expect your methods to be effective. If the parents can be helpful with a problem, this is a good place to ask for their cooperation.

3. **Encourage parents to participate in the conference.** After the parents have heard the report concerning their child's learning progress, they should be given an opportunity to make suggestions or ask questions. Some parents will talk at length, some will ask about specific points, and others may hesitate to participate at all. In the latter case, parent participation can be encouraged by asking open-ended questions rather than "yes-no" questions. For example, greater participation by the parents can be obtained by asking them "How does Mary feel about reading?" than by asking "Does Mary like reading?" Participation by the parents can also be encouraged by being an interested listener when the parent does talk.

4. **Be cautious about giving advice.** During parent-teacher conferences, some parents are likely to ask how to handle a specific home problem regarding the child. It might be a discipline problem, a problem concerning a child's allowance, or any of the other common problems of child rearing. Don't be a "know it all" and hand out pat answers. In most cases it is desirable to encourage the parents to work out the solution themselves. If any information is given, it should be presented in terms of a series of possible alternatives that have been tried by other parents with similar problems. In the final analysis, decisions concerning home child-rearing practices rest with the parents and this should be communicated to them. This, of course, does not rule out giving advice on educational matters (e.g., how to aid students with homework) or developing a cooperative program with parents for improving a student's learning and development.

Planning a Course of Action. The final phase of the conference involves summarizing the major points and planning a course of action. The following guidelines are useful for ending the conference in a purposeful way.

1. **Begin the concluding phase of the conference with a brief overall summary.** A summary of points made during the conference serves two purposes. It provides a clear signal to the parent that the conference is coming to an end and it sets the stage for planning a course of action. The summary should include a review of the student's strong points, the areas needing improvement, and any positive suggestions that have been made for helping the student.

2. Have parents participate in planning a course of action. In some cases, plans for helping the student evolve as a natural part of the interaction during the conference. Where this happens, the plans should be summarized as part of the overall summary and the parents should be asked to comment on their completeness and feasibility. Discussion at this point should focus on the specific steps that can be taken at home and school to help the student. If a course of action has not been discussed during the conference, it should be worked out cooperatively following the conference summary. For students making normal progress, this phase of the conference will be brief. For some problem cases, it may be necessary to make tentative plans and to arrange for another conference with the parents. This will enable you to keep to your scheduled time for each conference. Getting too far off schedule can antagonize those parents who are kept waiting beyond their appointed times.

3. Review your conference notes with parents. Ideally, a conference report form should be used that provides the parents with a copy of the conference notes (see Appendix B). If this is not possible, you should at least review your notes with the parents. This is probably best done during the summary of the conference. The parents might be asked, at the end of the review, if there is anything that they would like to have added to the notes.

4. End the conference on a positive note. At the conclusion of the conference, make some positive comments about the student, thank the parents for coming, and let them know that they are welcome to visit the school or call you at any time. At this point, some parents will want to continue the discussion or to bring up new topics. Be friendly and courteous, but tactfully remind them that your next scheduled appointment is due.

Some Important Conference "Don'ts"

A list of things to avoid during the parent-teacher conference has been presented by Bailard and Strang (1964) in the form of the following important "don'ts":

1. Don't put the parent on the defensive about anything.
2. Don't talk about other children or compare this child with other children. It is most unprofessional.
3. Don't talk about other teachers to the parents unless the remarks are of a complimentary nature.
4. Don't belittle the administration or make derogatory remarks about the school district.
5. Don't argue with the parent.
6. Don't try to outtalk a parent.
7. Don't interrupt the parent to make your own point.
8. Don't go too far with a parent who is not ready and able to understand your purpose.

9. Don't ask the parents personal questions which might be embarrassing to them. Only information pertinent to the child's welfare is important. Questions asked out of mere curiosity are unforgivable.

10. After the conference don't repeat any confidential information which the parent may volunteer. It is most unprofessional and can be very damaging to the parent or the child.

This list of "don'ts" provides useful guidelines for all contacts with parents, not just those during the parent-teacher conference.

Reporting Standardized Test Results to Parents

Special problems may be encountered when standardized test results are to be interpreted to parents during the parent-teacher conference. Unless the results are presented in simple language, which is meaningful to the parents, misunderstanding is likely to result. Because of the difficulty of communicating test results in understandable terms, some schools withhold this information from parents. This is undesirable, however, because standardized measures of scholastic aptitude and achievement provide parents with useful information for understanding their children's school progress and for assisting them with their educational and vocational plans.

In general, communicating meaningful test results to parents involves helping parents understand the following:

1. What did the tests measure?
2. What do the test scores mean?
3. How accurate are the test scores?
4. How is the test information to be used?

Although test interpretation need not follow the order of the questions, step-by-step, these are the basic considerations in explaining test scores to parents.

Describing What the Tests Measured. The description of the tests need not be elaborate and certainly should not be technical. In describing an intelligence or scholastic aptitude test, for example, you might simply say that the test measures "the ability to learn" or "the ability to do schoolwork." More elaborate explanations (e.g., "the test measures verbal and numerical abilities that are useful in schoolwork") might be used with some parents, but generally it should be kept as simple as possible. Typically, it is better not to refer to mental ability tests as intelligence tests. The term *intelligence* is frequently misunderstood by parents. Many parents tend to view it as a fixed, inherent quality that cannot be modified by experience. Since most test publishers have replaced the term *intelligence* in their test titles with such terms as *mental ability*, *scholastic aptitude*, and *academic potential*, use of the term *intelligence* is easily avoided.

In describing what achievement tests measure, the names of the subtests frequently provide a sufficient guide. To say that a reading test measures knowledge of vocabulary, speed of reading, and reading comprehension is sufficient for many purposes. In some cases, it may be desirable to describe the specific reading skills measured and to compare the test results with classroom performance. Similarly, with tests of arithmetic, language arts, science, and social studies, either the subtests can be used or the skills and content of the test can be described in greater detail. The important thing is to present only as much detail as is needed by the parents to make the report meaningful to them. Don't overwhelm them with elaborate test descriptions that cannot be grasped in the short span of time allotted to test interpretation.

Interpretations of interest inventories and personality inventories typically should not be made by teachers. If parents ask about such information, they should be referred to the director of guidance or the school principal.

Explaining What the Test Scores Mean. The scores used to report student performance on standardized tests should be simple, easy to grasp, and subject to a minimum of misinterpretation. In general, the following types of test scores should *not* be reported to parents for the reasons given.

1. IQ scores should not be reported to parents because they are likely to consider them a fixed and precise measure of mental ability; they are neither. The IQ is influenced by environmental factors, and IQ scores are subject to the same variation as are other test scores. Even under the most ideal testing conditions, an individual's IQ can be expected to vary from 5 to 10 points. If IQ scores are obtained from different tests, the variation will be even greater (Gronlund, 1971). To prevent misinterpretation, it is better to report mental ability test results in terms of other score units and to avoid the use of the term *intelligence* altogether.

2. Grade and age equivalents typically should not be used in reporting achievement test results to parents because they are so easily misunderstood. If a sixth-grade student earns a grade equivalent of 7.5 in arithmetic, for example, a parent is likely to believe that he is performing one year above his present grade placement. The parent might even feel that the child should be moved to a higher grade. A student can obtain a grade equivalent above his grade placement, however, by simply doing the lower level work more rapidly and accurately than the typical student. A one-year difference in grade equivalents is frequently represented by no more than 3 or 4 raw score points on the test; in some cases even less. A literal interpretation of grade and age equivalents by parents severely limits their value in describing the achievement of individual students. Other limitations of these units can be found in standard measurement textbooks (see Gronlund, 1971).

The two most useful methods of reporting standardized test results to parents are by means of (1) percentile ranks and (2) stanines. Both are easy to explain to parents and since both describe test performance in terms of relative position in some known group, misinterpretation is less likely to occur.

Percentile ranks describe test performance in terms of the percentage of students in some comparison group that earned an equal or lower score. Thus, in interpreting a percentile rank of 85 to a parent, it is simply a matter of pointing out that the student's performance equaled or surpassed 85 per cent of the students in the norm group. It is also important, of course, to describe the nature of the norm group (e.g., a national sample of sixth graders).

Two precautions should be taken in interpreting percentile ranks to parents. (1) Be sure they understand that percentile rank does *not* refer to the percentage of test items that the student answered correctly. (2) Make clear that percentile ranks do *not* provide a scale of equal units (i.e., a difference of a few percentile ranks represents a greater difference in test performance at the ends of the distribution than in the middle). Except for these two points, there is little chance for confusion or misunderstanding in reporting test results by means of percentile ranks.

Stanines describe test performance in terms of a nine-point scale of standard scores (STAndard NINES). The distribution of stanines and the percentage of students falling within each stanine are presented in Figure 6. Parents can quickly grasp the meaning of stanines if they are shown Figure 6 and given a brief explanation. Like percentile ranks, stanines report test performance in terms of the student's relative position in some known group. Unlike percentile ranks, however, only nine broad categories are used (rather than 0 to 100) so that test results are less likely to be overinterpreted.

STANINE	Description
9 (4%)	High (4%)
8 (7%) 7 (12%)	Above Average (19%)
6 (17%) 5 (20%) 4 (17%)	Average (54%)
3 (12%) 2 (7%)	Below Average (19%)
1 (4%)	Low (4%)

Figure 6. Percentage of students at each stanine level.

Stanines are becoming widely used with standardized tests, and many schools develop local norms based on the stanine scale. Besides being easily understood by parents, they provide a nonthreatening means of describing performance on a mental ability test and a good basis for comparing learning ability and achievement. Stanines are comparable from one type of test to another, provided that they are all based on the same norm group. Thus, a stanine of 7 on a mental ability test and a stanine of 5 on an achievement test would indicate a degree of underachievement. Typically, a difference of two or more stanines represents a significant difference in test performance.

The stanine system is described in greater detail by Gronlund (1968) and Lyman (1970). A series of questions and answers concerning the use of stanines in parent-teacher conferences is presented in a brief bulletin by Dursost (1961).

Clarifying the Lack of Accuracy in Test Scores. In interpreting test results to parents, it is important to communicate to them that all test scores are subject to error. In the case of percentile ranks, it is best to talk about the student's rank (e.g., 70 per cent) as an *estimate* that would probably be several points higher or lower on a second testing. If error bands are reported for the test, these, of course, can be used to show the margin of error surrounding each obtained score. Profiles of test scores using such error bands are provided by a number of test publishers (see Gronlund, 1971).

Where stanines are being used to report test scores, parents might be told that these broad units allow for lack of precision in testing. Classifying students into nine categories is about as precise as is warranted with many tests. As noted earlier, when comparing an individual's scores from different tests, a difference of two stanines typically represents a significant difference in test performance. A difference of one stanine is not regarded as significant, since a difference that small could be accounted for by errors of measurement alone. Thus, stanines provide a simple means of conveying to parents how to allow for error in test interpretation.

Discussing How the Test Information Is to Be Used. Interpreting test results to parents is not enough. This should be followed up with an explanation of how the test results are to be used in the instructional program (e.g., plan remedial work) and a discussion of specific actions that might be taken as a result of the test information. This discussion is likely to be most meaningful if it is an integral part of the general report on student learning progress. Use of the test results is then discussed along with other information in planning a course of action for helping the student improve his learning and development.

Check List for Evaluating a Marking and Reporting System

The marking and reporting system in any school must be in harmony with the objectives of the school program and with the needs of the users of the reports. Therefore, it would be impossible to describe a system that would be universally acceptable. It is possible, however, to list criteria for evaluating a marking and reporting system. Such criteria provide useful guidelines for improving marking and reporting practices. They are also helpful in understanding the characteristics of an effective reporting system.

CHECK LIST

Yes   No

Development of the Reporting System

1. Is there a clear statement of the purposes of the marking and reporting system? ____ ____
2. Was the system cooperatively developed by parents, students, teachers, and other school personnel? ____ ____
3. Is the system based on the objectives of the school program? ____ ____
4. Are the objectives understood and accepted by parents, students, and teachers? ____ ____
5. Are the objectives stated in measurable form? ____ ____
6. Can achievement of the objectives be validly and reliably evaluated by teachers? ____ ____
7. Have the needs of all intended users of the reports been considered? ____ ____
8. Does the system allow for different reporting practices at the elementary and secondary levels? ____ ____
9. Does the system provide for different reporting needs from one subject to another (e.g., science versus music)? ____ ____

Yes   No

10. Does the system provide for as much uniformity in the meaning of letter grades as is possible?   ____ ____

Nature of the Report Form

11. Is the report form brief, compact, and easy to use?   ____ ____
12. Are the symbols and procedures for marking clearly defined?   ____ ____
13. Do the letter grades for each subject (if used) represent a pure measure of achievement?   ____ ____
14. Is the standard for assigning letter grades (relative or absolute) clearly indicated?   ____ ____
15. Is diagnostic information for each subject included (e.g., check list of objectives)?   ____ ____
16. Is there a place to report on effort, personal and social characteristics, and work habits?   ____ ____
17. Does the report form encourage two-way communication between home and school?   ____ ____
18. Is the report form easily understood by parents, students, and other users?   ____ ____
19. Are parent-teacher conferences provided for, as needed?   ____ ____
20. Can the reports be easily summarized for school records?   ____ ____

Effects of the Reporting System

21. Does the system encourage teachers to evaluate all important outcomes of instruction?   ____ ____
22. Does the system have a positive influence on student learning and development?   ____ ____
23. Does the system contribute to student self-evaluation and self-understanding?   ____ ____
24. Does the system aid students in their educational and vocational planning?   ____ ____
25. Does the system promote good relations with parents and the general public?   ____ ____

Appendix B
Sample Parent-Teacher Conference Guide

Date _____ School _____

Parent's Name _____

Child's Name _____

Teacher _____ Grade _____

PLEASE
BRING THIS FORM
TO YOUR
SCHEDULED
CONFERENCE.
IT WILL BE YOUR
RECORD.

WINNETKA PUBLIC SCHOOLS
CONFERENCE GUIDE AND RECORD FOR PARENTS AND TEACHERS
Grades I and II

We are sending this combination guide and record as a convenience for you in looking forward to our conference. We urge you to go over the following pages carefully to see how you can contribute to our conference and to be informed concerning areas of progress your child's teacher will be evaluating.

This form has been made inclusive to cover items of concern in the total school program. Some of the topics will be more relevant to your child than others. If some thought is given before the conference to those that relate to your child, we can move along more expeditiously when we get together.

Your conference is scheduled for _____ at _____ o'clock

in _____.

Sincerely yours,

COOPERATIVE ACTION AGREED UPON IN OUR CONFERENCE

_____ to continue present program unchanged

_____ to pursue the following plan: (date each agreement separately as developed during the year)

You are invited to select from the following topics those that seem important to you for helping us to understand your child better. A space is provided for you to record essential information for use during the conference and for subsequent reference immediately after the conference.

TOPICS	PARENTS' NOTES Before and after conference
1. How does your child enjoy going to school? What does he say about school, his teacher, other children? Does he tell about what he does in school?	
2. How does he get along with family members; with playmates?	
3. Does he accept routines easily? (bedtime, mealtime, stopping play, putting away toys, etc.)	
4. How does he accept new situations? (with ease, easily upset)	
5. Does he have some regular responsibilities at home?	
6. Is he developing self-discipline? (accepts controls easily, cooperates willingly). What kinds of controls do you use?	
7. Is he developing good health habits, getting regular and sufficient sleep, eating wisely and adequately, learning personal grooming? Does he have some physical difficulty we should be aware of?	
8. Does he have any special interests? What does he like to do at home?	
9. Are there other things about your child we should know? Are new developments occurring that should be brought to our attention? Do you have any suggestions to help us in guiding your child?	

Name _____ Teacher _____ Date _____

As your child's teacher, I am preparing to discuss the following aspects of his growth in school with you.

ACADEMIC PROGRESS	
SUBJECTS	**NOTES** Before and After Conference
WORK HABITS: Does he listen attentively? Does he follow directions? Does he work carefully and accurately without disturbing others? Does he complete work in a reasonable amount of time? Does he make constructive use of free time?	
READING AND LANGUAGE:	
ARITHMETIC:	
SOCIAL STUDIES:	
HANDWRITING:	
SCIENCE:	

GROWTH AS AN INDIVIDUAL: Does he assume responsibility? Use good judgment? Show initiative? Does he respect rules, authority, personal and public property? Does he show a questioning mind? Is his work self-motivated? Is he adjustable to change? Does he feel responsible for putting forth his best efforts?	
GROWTH AS GROUP MEMBER: Does he participate in group activities? Does he cooperate and get along well with others? Respect the rights of others? Does he contribute to group discussions? Does he show willingness to serve both as a leader and as a follower? Is he learning the obligations and practices of citizenship in a democracy?	

Note: Pages 1-4 to be used for initial conference annually. For subsequent conferences, **pages 3 and 4 will be furnished in** blank to the parent, and will be completed for the cumulative file by the teacher.

Appendix C
References

Bailard, Virginia, and Ruth Strang. *Parent-Teacher Conferences.* New York: McGraw-Hill, 1964.

Cureton, Louise W. "The History of Grading Practices," *Measurement in Education.* East Lansing, Mich.: National Council on Measurement in Education, 1971.

Dursost, W. N. *How to Tell Parents About Standardized Test Results.* Test Service Notebook, No. 26. New York: Harcourt, 1961.

Gronlund, N. E. *Constructing Achievement Tests.* Englewood Cliffs, N.J.: Prentice-Hall, 1968.

——— *Stating Behavioral Objectives for Classroom Instruction.* New York: Macmillan, 1970.

——— *Measurement and Evaluation in Teaching.* 2d ed. New York: Macmillan, 1971.

——— *Preparing Criterion-Referenced Tests for Classroom Instruction.* New York: Macmillan, 1973.

——— *Individualizing Classroom Instruction.* New York: Macmillan, 1974.

Lyman, H. B. *Test Scores and What They Mean.* Englewood Cliffs, N.J.: Prentice-Hall, 1970.

Millman, J. "Reporting Student Progress: A Case for a Criterion-Referenced Marking System," *Phi Delta Kappan,* 52, 226–230, 1970.

Mousley, W. "Report Cards Across the Nation," *Phi Delta Kappan,* 53, 436–437, 1972.

National Education Association. "Marking and Reporting Pupil Progress," *Research Summary 1970 S-1.* Washington, D.C.: NEA Research Division 1970.

Terwilliger, J. S. "Self-Reported Marking Practices and Policies in Public Secondary Schools," *Bulletin of the National Association of Secondary-School Principals,* 50, 5–37, 1966.

Terwilliger, J. S. *Assigning Grades to Students*. Glenview, Ill.: Scott, Foresman, 1971.

Thorndike, R. L. "Marks and Marking Systems," in R. L. Ebel (ed.), *Encyclopedia of Educational Research*, 4th ed., New York: Macmillan, 1969.

Williams, R. G., and H. G. Miller. "Grading Students: A Failure to Communicate," *Clearing House*, 47, 332–337, 1973.

Wrinkle, W. L. *Improving Marking and Reporting Practices*. New York: Holt, 1947.

Index

Achievement measurement, 13, 22, 30

Check list, 49
Check lists of objectives, 3, 6, 19, 28
Combining data, 23-24
Criterion-referenced marking
  and conventional grading, 31-32
  defined, 14-16
  examples of, 34, 36
  and individualized instruction, 35-37
  and mastery learning, 32-35
  problems of, 29-31

Dual marking, 17, 18, 27

Effort, 13, 16, 17, 18, 19

Functions of marking, 10-13

Goal card, 36
Grade distributions, 25-27
Grading on normal curve, 25-26
Guidelines
  for marking and reporting, 19-20
  for parent-teacher conference, 39-43

Individualized instruction, 31, 35-37

Letter grades
  advantages and limitations of, 5
  assigning criterion-referenced, 31-33
  assigning norm-referenced, 21-27
  considerations in using, 1
  distribution of, 25-27
  supplementing, 27-28
  use on report forms, 16-20
  validity, 22
Letters to parents, 6

Marking and reporting
  criterion-referenced, 14-16, 29-37
  distribution of grades, 25-27
  factors in, 13-14
  functions of, 10-13
  guidelines for improving, 19-20
  norm-referenced, 14-16, 21-28
  trends in, 7
  types of, 3, 4, 5-7, 16-19

Mastery learning, 31, 32-35
Multiple marking and reporting
  examples of, 17, 18
  factors in, 13, 27-28
  guidelines for, 19-20

Norm-referenced marking
  and achievement, 22
  combining data for, 23-25
  defined, 14-16
  grade distributions, 25-27
  grading on the curve, 25
  supplementing grades, 27-28
Normal curve, 26

Objectives, 3, 6, 19, 28

Parent-teacher conference
  advantages and limitations, 6-7
  conducting, 40-43
  don'ts, 43-44
  establishing rapport, 40-41
  guide, 52-55
  planning course of action, 42-43
  preparing for, 39-40
  sharing information, 41-42
Pass-fail system, 5, 8, 12, 27
Percentile ranks, 46
Personal characteristics, 14, 17, 18, 19
Promotion, 27

Rapport, 40
Report cards
  examples of, 17, 18, 34, 36
  guidelines for, 19-20
  in current use, 3, 4
Reporting standardized test results, 44-47
Retention, 27

Standards for marking
  absolute, 14-16, 21, 30, 31
  relative, 14-16, 21, 25-28
Stanines, 46

Test scores, 45-47
Trends in marking, 7

Weighting composite scores, 23-24
Work habits, 14, 17, 18, 19